THE NEW CHINESE-KOSHER COOKBOOK

THE NEW CHINESE-KOSHER COOKBOOK

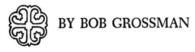 BY BOB GROSSMAN

PAUL S. ERIKSSON
Publisher
Middlebury, Vermont

Library of Congress Cataloging in Publication Data

Grossman, Bob.
    The new Chinese-kosher cookbook.

    Revision of the 1963 edition by R. and B. Grossman published under title: The Chinese-kosher cookbook.
    Includes index.
    1. Cookery, Jewish. 2. Cookery, Chinese.
I. Grossman, Ruth. The Chinese-kosher cookbook.
II. Title.
TX724.G729   1978   641.5′67   77-79248
ISBN 0-8397-6308-5
ISBN 0-8397-6309-3 pbk.

*To Grandmother Slipakoff
who held her first pair of
chopsticks at eighty*

Thou shalt not eat any abominable thing . . .

And every beast that parteth the hoof, and cleaveth the cleft into two claws, and chewest the cud among beasts, that ye shall eat . . .

These ye shall eat of all that are in the waters: all that have fins and scales shall ye eat . . .

Of all clean birds ye shall eat . . .

But these are they of which ye shall not eat: the eagle, the ossifrage and the osprey . . . and the glede, and the kite, and the vulture after his kind,

And every raven after his kind . . .

And every creeping thing that flieth is unclean unto you: they shall not be eaten . . .

But of all clean fowls ye may eat . . .

Ye shall not eat of any thing that dieth of itself . . . thou shalt not seethe a kid in his mother's milk . . .

DEUTERONOMY XIV

CONTENTS

PREFACE

Chinese cooking in America has come a long way since *The Chinese-Kosher Cookbook* was written in 1963. Although the Cantonese cuisine is still offered by a majority of our Chinese restaurants, many other restaurants are devoting themselves to the foods of other provinces. Unusual ingredients, pungent aromas and fiery spices create an interest in Chinese food that is unparalleled in American culinary habits. Best known of this new variety of foods are the dishes of Szechuan and Hunan. They are as different from Cantonese food as French is from Mexican. Garlic, ginger and fresh or dried chili peppers are to be found in these dishes in profusion. The result, given that one has the stomach for it, is a unique and memorable combination of flavors that tend to be addictive.

With this in mind, I believe that *The Chinese-Kosher Cookbook* should reflect some of the newly discovered dishes of these provinces. For those of you who keep a kosher home and enjoyed the past excursion into Chinese food I hope you will also venture a bit further and sample some of my new recipes. For those of you who are "not so kosher," and are familiar with Szechuan and Hunan food, I can only wish you a "hearty appetite" and that you'll find these recipes as good and authentic as those of your favorite Chinese restaurant.

"Eat and be well!"

Bob Grossman

Middletown, New Jersey

PREFACE TO FIRST EDITION

Friday night is a big night in a Jewish home. It is the beginning of the Sabbath and it is usually the time when that part of the family which has moved away, through marriage, or a desire to live a bachelor's existence in the Big City, is cajoled and coerced to "come over, you should have a nice, hot meal with the family."

But after being exposed to the epicurian delights of some of the most wonderful restaurants in the world, we began to hesitate about the delicious, but routine chicken or roast beef of Friday night. Ruth's grandmother (who lives in Louisiana, of all places!) cooks exactly the same dishes in exactly the same manner as Bob's grandmother (who lives in Brooklyn, of all places!). So no amount of, "What's the matter, you forgot maybe the address?" or, "You can bring even the poodle if he stays already under the table," could deter us from our favorite food at wonderful Chinese restaurants we had discovered all over the world . . . from Hong Kong to Tel Aviv.

So one day, Grandmother Slipakoff said, "All right, you'll come over Friday night, I'll cook Chow Mein."

We went over that fateful evening, more out of admiration for Grandma's sense of humor than with anticipation of having a Chinese meal . . . we knew we'd get chicken or roast beef or even chopped liver served with a Chinese name. But what to our wondering eyes should appear but Grandma's first attempt at acknowledging the 20th Century! Won Ton Soup ("so good the *Rebitsen* could eat it")—Jewish Chow Mein, and for dessert, the age old Chinese restaurant favorite: pineapple chunks pierced with toothpicks.

Grandmother Slipakoff, now 82, has a favorite Jewish expression: *"As men lebt, d'lebt men alles."* (As I live, I see everything.) And we felt we'd seen everything. So Grandmother Slipakoff got everyone she could—the neighbors, her own children, the seltzer man— to collect Chinese recipes . . . and with her great natural talent as a cook, she figured out a way to make her grandchildren's favorite dishes Kosher, so she could cook them and there'd be no excuse for our not coming over to dinner each time we were asked.

We still enjoy the traditional Jewish dishes we grew up with . . . but we know the world of Jewish cooking will never be the same. We thought we'd truly seen everything, until one day: Grandma asked us to take her to Chinatown . . . and there, as we stood in back of a little shop with our mouths open in amazement, Grandma Slipakoff bought two pairs of chopsticks . . . one *fleischig* . . . and one *milchig*!

Truly: *As men lebt, d'lebt men alles!*

Ruth & Bob Grossman

Brooklyn Heights, N. Y.

THE NEW CHINESE-KOSHER
COOKBOOK

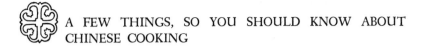 A FEW THINGS, SO YOU SHOULD KNOW ABOUT
CHINESE COOKING

There are a few things, that maybe you should know, so you can be a real "mayvin" of Chinese cooking.

First and most important is timing. This doesn't mean you have to break your neck, rushing around the kitchen. It just means that you've got to think ahead.

The ingredients you use are sliced nice and thin, or chopped up fine so they cook nice and even all over and also fast. You'll be smart if you prepare all ingredients before you even put a pot on the stove. These you can put in little bowls so they'll be ready when you need them. This will prevent all the "tsurris" of burning food and sliced thumbs. (You shouldnt know from it!)

Most of the recipes that you'll see in this book will call for a little frying. This doesn't mean regular frying, it means what they call in Hong Kong, "stir-frying." A little oil you should put in the frying pan and when it's good and hot, then you can throw in the ingredients. Keep high the fire and just fry and stir, fry and stir, fry and stir. In a minute or two it'll be done. This trick keeps the food from burning and makes sure that all the pieces are evenly cooked. It also is very healthy, you don't soak out the vitamins and all the healthy juices are sealed in.

Deep-frying is already another method of preparing Chinese food. For this, a deep-fryer, or just a pot oil will be perfect. For a rule of "sliced" thumb, when the oil bubbles a little it's about right for fish and chicken. When it smokes, then it's good for beef.

Also, we shouldn't forget to tell you, peanut oil or other vegetable oil is very good to fry in. (And it's Kosher yet!)

When the recipe calls for meat, make sure it's good and lean—not that fat stuff the butcher tries to get rid of. If you need sliced

3

meat, the best thing to do is to freeze the meat a little. This will make it easy to cut into thin slices. When you're through slicing, they should measure about 2" x 1" and be ⅛" thick. When the recipe calls for slivers or shreds, then you can cut the meat into pieces like matchsticks. Another thing to remember, always cut against the grain. Also, you should cut off all the gristle.

Onions and mushrooms cut straight. Other vegetables cut a little slanty. When you cut slanty, each piece has more surface open and you'll see already how much faster it cooks.

Most of the items used in these recipes you know. Other things, like soy sauce, which is made from soy beans and is brown and salty, might be new to you; but you shouldn't be without it! This, together with bamboo shoots, water chestnuts, and bean sprouts you can find in almost any supermarket. MSG, which is monosodium glutamate, is used to bring out the "tamm" in all foods. It is a white powder made from wheat flour. It's sold under a lot of different brand names. (Listen, it's wonderful even when you're not cooking Chinese food.)

You'll see in these recipes duck sauce and mustard. Duck sauce, so you shouldn't worry, doesn't have duck in it. It contains peaches, apricots and other fruits with vinegar, salt, sugar and spices. You'll find it in any grocery; and mustard you'll mix yourself from a little dry mustard and water.

So Mazeltuv! Now you know a few things about Chinese cooking. You should live and be well!

4

YOU'RE USING MAYBE CHOPSTICKS?

This maybe will help you get the idea. First you should place one chopstick in the round hollow between your thumb and your index finger and rest its lower end below the first joint of the third finger. This chopstick doesn't move. Hold the other chopstick between the tips of the index and middle fingers, making steady its upper half against the bottom of the index finger, using the tip of the thumb to keep it already in place. To pick up things, move the upper chopstick with index and middle fingers. So your food shouldn't get cold while you're learning, maybe practice with the forshpeis. Have plenty of napkins—and plenty guests with a good sense of humor.

Zei Gezint!

TEA EGGS OY VAZE MEER*

12 eggs
3 cups boiling water
1 teaspoon anise seed
¼ cup soy sauce
5 tablespoons orange pekoe tea
1 tablespoon salt

Boil the eggs for 10 minutes so they should be hard. Take them out from the water and chill by putting them in cold water. Then you can take off from them the shells. Put in a pot the anise seed, soy sauce, tea and salt and pour over them from the kettle the 3 cups boiling water. Put in this the eggs and simmer nice for 1 hour. Now you can chill them and serve for a forshpeis. You'll have a surprise when you see the new color of the eggs.

* OY VAZE MEER: what you say when you realize you just buttered the bagel with a meat knife!

8

FISH BALLS TZATZ KELL LAH*

1 lb. flounder filet
10 water chestnuts
2 tablespoons cornstarch
2 tablespoons sherry
A couple pinches salt
1 nice egg
A pot hot oil

The fish chop up nice and fine (a blender is easier, if you have one); also the water chestnuts. This you'll mix together and also add the cornstarch, sherry, salt and the beaten up egg. When it's all mixed together already, you'll make from it little balls about ¾ or an inch big. Make hot the pot oil and fry the balls until they get a nice golden brown. Serve it with hot mustard and duck sauce.

* TZATZ KELL LAH: what a Jewish child thinks is its first name.

EGG ROLL HAH DAH SAH*

FOR FLAT PANCAKES:

2 cups flour   A cup and a half water
A pinch salt   2 nice eggs
A pot full of fat so you can fry

First you should mix together everything but the fat until it's smooth. Take a small frying pan, about six inches, and put a little oil in it. Then you should pour some of the batter and let it spread over the whole pan. Watch out, it shouldn't get too hot. When it looks ready on one side, turn it over for a few seconds on the other. When that's done, put it on the side and make another. Do this a lot of times until you use up all the stuff.

NOW YOU'LL MAKE THE STUFFING:

A nice breast chicken cooked   2 tablespoons soy sauce
A couple pinches salt   1 little can mushrooms
A couple pinches sugar   1 cup bean sprouts
1 teaspoon cornstarch   A few chopped scallions
2 tablespoons oil or schmaltz   ½ cup sliced onion
¼ cup bamboo shoots

The chicken should be cut into tiny pieces, but not too tiny. Mix it up with the salt, the sugar, the cornstarch and the soy sauce. Then let it stand. You'll come back in a minute.

Now take a tablespoon oil or schmaltz in a deep frying pan and put in the mushrooms, bean sprouts, scallions, onion and bamboo shoots. This you should sauté for a couple minutes. Then you'll put in the chicken and the stuff it's soaking in. Cook it for another couple minutes and let it cool.

When it's cooled enough, so you shouldn't get burned, you'll take a nice big tablespoon full and put it in the middle of one of the flat latkes you made before. Roll it like you are making a long thin package. To seal, brush with a beaten egg. Then do the rest.

Get the pot full of fat nice and hot (375°) and fry a few pieces at a time. You'll know that when it gets brown, you should take it out. Let it drain before you serve it.

On the table you should have some hot mustard, and some duck sauce. Also, a very good sauce for this is apple-sauce mixed with hot white horseradish. Chinese this sauce isn't, but it's good. This makes 8 to 10 delicious pieces.

* HAH DAH SAH: the Jewish answer to the D.A.R.

FOH NEE SHRIMP PUFFS*

One jar gefillte fish balls
One pot hot oil

Get the pot oil good and hot and put in the gefillte fish balls. Let them get a nice healthy brown and they're finished. Take them out from the oil, stick in them toothpicks and serve. Duck sauce and mustard is nice to dip in.

FOH NEE SHRIMP TOAST*

FOR THIS DELICACY, AGAIN YOU'LL NEED
A POT HOT OIL. ALSO:

1 lb. flounder filet	A little salt
3 or 4 scallions	A little pepper
4 tablespoons soy sauce	Triangles of white bread

Take the fish, and chop it up, or put it in a blender. Mix in some chopped scallions, the soy sauce, salt and pepper. Shmear this on the pieces bread and cook it in the hot oil until it gets nice and brown. This is also good with duck sauce and mustard. It makes a nice forshpeis and a better heartburn. (Makes about 12 shtichlach).

* Not even from a *modern* Kosher Grandmother should you expect real shrimp!

12

STUFFED MUSHROOMS
MAH ZEL TUV*

20 nice large mushrooms
¾ lb. ground meat
3 tablespoons chopped scallions
3 tablespoons soy sauce
A few pinches salt
A little pinch pepper
1 tablespoon flour
1 cup beef or chicken broth

Wash the mushrooms nice and put away the stems for something else. Chop up together the meat and scallions they should be very fine. Now mix in a tablespoon soy sauce, salt, pepper and flour. Shape this into small balls and into the mushrooms you'll stuff. Now in a large frying pan you'll pour in the rest of the soy sauce and the broth. Put in the mushrooms with the stuffed side up, and put on the pan a cover, and for 20 minutes you should cook. If it's not done, don't worry, you'll cook a little more. This is a delicious forshpeis for Bar Mitzvahs, weddings, or Bris receptions.

* *MAH ZEL TUV:* what they told Columbus when he got back to Spain.

FRIED WON TON REB EH TSIN*

First comes the kreplach (also called won ton; also called ravioli—depending on your neighborhood).

FOR THE STUFFING YOU'LL TAKE:

A little schmaltz or oil   1 onion chopped
½ lb. chopped meat   2 pinches salt
A pinch pepper

Heat in the frying pan a little schmaltz or oil and put in the meat and onions. You'll cook for a few minutes until it's brown. Now put in the salt and pepper. Next, it should cool.

FOR THE DOUGH:

A cup and a half flour   2 tablespoons water
A pinch salt   1 fresh egg

Sift the flour together with the salt into a bowl. Then you'll blend in the egg and water. Put this on a table covered with a little flour and knead it smooth. Now cover it up and leave it for 10 minutes. Then with a rolling pin you'll roll it very thin. Cut it up into pieces 3 inches square. In each square, you'll put a little stuffing and fold it like a triangle. Squeeze the edges together and cook it in salted water for 15 minutes.

NOW YOU'LL TAKE:

2 tablespoons oil	1 teaspoon soy sauce
⅔ cup chopped onion	¾ cup beef or chicken broth
1 tablespoon cornstarch	A pot full of hot fat

Take the won ton and when the fat, it gets hot, put them in and fry on both sides. They should get brown. This should take about 10-15 minutes. Then put them on paper towels to drain off the oil. Take 2 tablespoons oil in a frying pan and cook in it the onions until tender and soft. While this cooks, mix together the cornstarch, soy sauce and broth. When the onions are ready pour in the mixture and mix up nice. Let it get good and thick and pour it over the fried won ton. This will serve about 4 people who, we'll make you a guarantee, will lick their fingers, especially if you forget to serve forks or chopsticks.

* REB EH TSIN: such a job for a nice Jewish girl!

15

HELZEL HONG KONG*

For this you should make a stuffing like for the EGG ROLL HAH DAH SAH (see page 10). But only half as much. Then take the neck skins from 3 or 4 chickens. (It depends if they have long necks or short necks.) With a needle and thread you should sew up one end of the neck, push in the stuffing and sew up the other end. Do this until you run out of necks or out of the stuffing. Next you should make hot a pot oil and fry the helzel until it looks like two weeks in Miami. Slice it in pieces and serve.

* HELZEL: the part of the chicken that if it gets wrung, it's not Kosher.

16

SMOKED BEEF BALLS PUSH KEH*

1-inch piece ginger	2 tablespoons cornstarch
2 nice scallions	A good pinch salt
2 lbs. ground beef	1 teaspoon sesame oil
4 tablespoons black soy	4 tablespoons brown sugar
6 star anise, broken up	

Chop up good the ginger and scallions and mix together with the beef, soy, cornstarch, salt and sesame oil. Now make little meatballs about the size of a walnut. Into a boiling pot water put in a few balls at a time. When they are all in, put on the cover and let them cook for 20 minutes. After this, you'll drain. Now get a big heavy pot and line it all over with foil. Leave enough foil sticking out so you can pinch it together so a cover it makes. Sprinkle on the foil the brown sugar and the star anise and put an old saucer on the bottom of the pot. Now the meatballs you'll put on a pan and the pan you'll put on the saucer in the pot. Bring together the ends of the foil and a few times you'll fold so it's nice and tight. Turn on the fire and let it smoke for 8-10 minutes. When you're done, tear the foil a little so the smoke should escape. Now it's ready to serve either hot or cold and also makes a nice snack. Enough you'll have for 6 people and if they dip in a little Szechuan Salt they'll love it!

* *PUSH KEH*: A Jewish Safety-Deposit Box.

PUNGENT CHICKEN WINGS
FAR CHAH DET*

12 chicken wings	1 tablespoon sugar
1 cup water	A teaspoon 5 Spices Powder
3 tablespoons black soy	1 tablespoon Hoi Sin sauce
A little splash sherry	

Put first the wings into a wok and then you'll add the water, black soy, sugar, 5 Spices Powder, Hoi Sin sauce and sherry. This you'll cook with a cover for about 30 minutes or until the wings look done. Every once in a while you should stir the wings so they'll all get covered with sauce. If, near the end, the sauce looks a little thin, take off the cover for a little while, it should get thicker. This you can serve hot or cold 4-6 people they'll lick their fingers.

* *FAR CHAH DET:* What Marvin was when the cash was put into the envelope addressed to the IRS and his tax return was mailed to the Swiss bank.

18

HOT AND COLD CHICKEN
FAR POTCH KET*

2 whole breasts chicken
3 cloves chopped garlic
1 tablespoon ginger, chopped
1 tablespoon sherry
4 tablespoons light soy

4 tablespoons cold tea
1 teaspoon chili paste with garlic
A teaspoon cornstarch in a little
water
2 scallions, chopped

Take off from the breasts the skin and then you'll put them into a bowl for steaming. Throw in the garlic, ginger, sherry, soy sauce and tea. Now put the bowl into a steamer (a covered wok is good for this) and you'll steam for 30 minutes. After the breasts are nice and tender take them out from the bowl so they'll cool. Next, you should put the sauce that's left into a wok and throw in the chili paste with garlic and you'll cook for a minute. Then the cornstarch with water you can add so the sauce gets a little thick. Now mix in the chopped scallions. By this time the chicken has cooled so you shouldn't burn the fingers. Take off from the bones the meat. Try to keep the breasts as whole as possible. When all the meat is off, with a sharp knife you'll cut it into bite-size pieces and put it nice on a serving plate. Pour over this the sauce and you can serve it cold to 4-6 people for an appetizing forspeis!

* FAR POTCH KET: Aunt Selma's description of a Jackson Pollack painting.

SOUPS

BUB UH LUH WON
TON SOUP*

For this you'll make kreplach just like for the FRIED WON
TON REB EH TSIN (see page 14).

THEN YOU'LL MAKE THE SOUP:

4 cups nice chicken broth
½ cup cooked chicken shreds
½ cup celery chopped
A few pieces lettuce, watercress or spinach

Boil first the broth; then put in the chicken and the greens;
also the kreplach. Let it boil for another minute and you
can serve it even to a Mandarin, it's so good. Serves 4
Mandarins.

* *BUB UH LUH*: proposed name of the first Israeli atomic sub-
marine.

22

CUCUMBER SOUP GAY AH VEK*

    4 cups nice chicken broth
  10 sliced mushrooms
    1 small can bamboo shoots
  ½ cup cooked chicken shreds
    1 teaspoon soy sauce
  A pinch salt or two
    1 teaspoon cornstarch
    1 fat cucumber

Put in a pot the chicken broth, mushrooms, bamboo shoots, chicken shreds, soy sauce, salt and the cornstarch mixed in a little water. Then you'll light the fire and simmer for 20 minutes. While you're simmering, peel already the cucumber and cut it in pieces about ½ inch thick. When the soup has simmered for 20 minutes, put in the cucumber pieces and boil for 3 or 4 minutes. Serve it right away, it shouldn't get cold. 4 people this serves.

* GAY AH VEK: Mother, please! I'd rather do it myself!

CHICKEN MUSHROOM
SOUP YID DIH SHA MAH MAH*

4 cups chicken broth	4 large mushrooms
1 small chopped onion	1 oz. egg noodles
1 teaspoon MSG	A few pieces lettuce, or water- cress

Put in the pot the broth and onion and MSG. Bring to a nice boil and throw in the sliced mushrooms and the egg noodles. Let it boil for another 10 minutes or so, put in then the pieces lettuce or watercress and serve. Serves 4 people. In China, it is known as Moo Goo Gai Tong; in Chinese restaurants, it is generally known as the one from Group A.

* YID DIH SHA MAH MAH: packs for her son, the astronaut, a thermos of hot chicken soup.

23

FAR BLUN JED EGG DROP SOUP*

3 cups nice chicken broth
1 tablespoon soy sauce
A pinch salt or two
A teaspoon MSG
1 nice fresh egg
A little handful watercress
2 teaspoons cornstarch
2 tablespoons water

In a pot you'll heat the broth to a boil. Then add the soy sauce, salt and MSG. Make a thin mixture of the cornstarch with the water and add this to the soup and cook until it thickens slightly. Next you can beat the egg and add it to the soup very slowly; all the time you should mix. Take it off from the fire, add the watercress and serve.

* FAR BLUN JED is what a Jewish mother calls her son when he wants to join the "Moonies" instead of becoming a doctor.

25

EGG FLOWER SOUP PAY SAH DIK*

4 cups nice rich chicken broth
½ cup celery sliced
½ onion chopped
A few pinches salt
1 fresh egg
A handful lettuce, spinach, or watercress

In a pot, you should boil the broth. Next throw in the celery, onion and salt. When it boils again, you'll mix up the egg and stir it in. When you're through stirring, put in the lettuce or spinach in pieces and let it cook for a minute. It's a very nice soup for Pesach and it will serve 4 people.

* PAY SAH DIK: refers to the Jewish holiday when the carpets of America are blanketed with matzoh crumbs—from wall to wall.

LUCK SHEN SOUP*

¾ lb. egg noodles already cooked
1 tablespoon soy sauce
2 tablespoons schmaltz
A few pinches salt
1½ cups sliced chicken

1 cup mushrooms
½ cup bean sprouts
1 cup water chestnuts sliced
1 tablespoon cornstarch
½ cup water
4 cups chicken broth

Divide the noodles into serving bowls and put in each a little soy sauce. Melt the schmaltz in a frying pan, put in a little salt and brown the slices chicken. Then put in the mushrooms, bean sprouts and water chestnuts. Blend the cornstarch with a little water and also put in. Cover the pot and cook until the vegetables soften a bit and the sauce thickens. In another pot make hot the broth and pour on the noodles. Now you can put in each bowl some of the chicken and vegetable mixture. If your bowls are the same size as ours, you'll serve 4 people. If they are smaller, maybe you'll squeeze out for 6 people.

* LUCK SHEN is what the Italians, Jews and Chinese all claim to have invented—actually, it's Tahitian!

27

HOT AND SOUR SOUP
AY BEEM*

3 dried mushrooms
8 tree ear mushrooms (fungus)
A tablespoon oil
A tablespoon soy sauce, light
A nice breast chicken, shredded
½ cup shredded bamboo shoots
5 cups nice chicken broth
A tablespoon black soy

A pinch salt
3 tablespoons wine vinegar
3 tablespoons water
2 tablespoons corn starch
2 beaten up eggs
A tablespoon sesame oil
A teaspoon white pepper
2 scallions, chopped

Put first the 2 kinds mushrooms in boiling water for 15 minutes. Wait so they'll get cool and cut off from the big mushrooms the stems, you shouldn't put in. Now, in the wok, you'll put the oil and light soy and cook for a minute or two the chicken shreds. Then the mushrooms and the bamboo shoots you should add and cook for a minute. The chicken broth you'll put with the black soy, salt and the vinegar into the wok and let simmer for a few minutes. Meanwhile, together the cornstarch and water you'll mix and then stir into the soup. When it gets a little thick and boils nice, turn off the fire and stir in the eggs. When the eggs are all cooked in the soup, mix in the sesame oil and pepper (you shouldn't sneeze). Sprinkle on the scallions and you'll be ready to serve for about 6 people, they should live and be well.

* AY BEEM: A New York City Mayor who would have grown a few more inches if his mother fed him this instead of chicken soup.

HOT POT GAN EDEN*

3 pounds nice boned lamb	½ cup wine vinegar
½ pound spinach, cleaned and rinsed	½ cup Hot Oil
	½ cup sesame oil
½ celery cabbage, in bite size pieces	½ cup red bean sauce
	½ cup cold tea
3 squares white bean curd	½ cup sesame paste
1 lb. fresh mushrooms, halved	2 tablespoons sugar
2 quarts chicken broth	½ cup light soy

Freeze first a little the lamb and then you can slice thin like a piece paper. Spread this out on a big plate and on table you'll put it. Also, you'll put on platters the spinach, celery cabbage, chunks of bean curd and the mushrooms. Now you can make hot on the table a fondue pot and cook to a boil the broth. While the broth, it's getting hot, mix up good together in the bowl the wine vinegar, Hot Oil, sesame oil, red bean sauce, tea, sesame paste, sugar and light soy. This will be the sauce you'll dip in. When the broth boils nice, each guest will take a little piece meat and hold in the broth with a fork or chopsticks for a minute or two until they cook. Now they can dip in the sauce and eat. After they get a little tired of meat they can cook a piece celery cabbage, or spinach or bean curd or whatever. Each piece can be dipped in the sauce. A nice thing about this is you can use all kinds vegetables or even meats and it's still good. It makes enough for six people and if anyone is still hungry he can mix up some broth in a bowl with the sauce and really have a picnic!

* GAN EDEN: A Miami Beach retirement community.

RICE, EGG, MATZOH
& NOODLE DISHES

YUN TIF FRIED RICE*

2 tablespoons oil	A little chopped celery
1 big onion chopped	A little chopped green pepper
½ cup chopped leftover chicken	3 cups leftover rice
	2 fresh eggs
½ cup chopped leftover meat	1 tablespoon soy sauce
A few pinches salt (maybe)	

Take a big frying pan, put in the oil it should get hot. Then fry the onion a little. Next, throw in the chicken, the meat and the vegetables. Then, you'll throw in the rice; give it once in a while a mix, until the whole thing gets a little brown. Now you should make a little hole in the middle so the pan shows through. Stir up the eggs and pour them in the hole. When the eggs begin to fry a little, you should begin mixing up the whole thing. Also, pour in the spoon soy sauce and maybe a little salt if it needs. When it looks finished, it is. Serves maybe 5 or 6.

* *YUN TIF:* any holiday when you have to kiss all the relatives and Mom brings out the shnapps.

32

TUH MEL FRIED RICE WITH MUSHROOMS*

2 nice fresh eggs	4 cups cooked cold rice
3 tablespoons oil	2 teaspoons soy sauce
½ lb. mushrooms	A few pinches salt
1 medium onion chopped	A little pepper

Beat up the eggs and put in a frying pan a little oil. When the oil gets hot add the eggs and cook like a latke (pancake). This you'll cut into thin strips. Add in the pan a little more oil and throw in the onion, it should cook till it's tender. Then put in the rest of the oil and add the rice and the pieces egg. Mix together the soy sauce, salt, pepper and throw it also in. Cook over a medium fire until it all gets hot and serve right away. This is a good way to use up leftover rice. Serves 4 people.

* TUH MEL: the family reunion to celebrate when Grandma got her "citizen's papers."

VEGETABLE OMLET GIB AH KEEK*

1 nice onion
4 mushrooms
1 green pepper
3 sticks celery
3 tablespoons oil
5 fresh eggs
A few pinches salt
A little pinch pepper

Chop up the onion, make the mushrooms in slices and in pieces you'll cut the pepper. Also the celery you'll cut into tiny pieces. Now you can heat up a frying pan and put in the oil. When it gets hot you'll throw in the onions and let them get a golden brown. Then the other vegetables you can throw in and cook for about a minute. When it's done, from the pan you should take them out and drain. Now beat up the eggs and mix them in with the vegetables, salt and pepper. Put in a little more oil in the pan and fry nice the egg and vegetable mixture on a low fire until it's set. This you can cut up into pieces and serve.

* *GIB AH KEEK* means—look at the size of that diamond!

34

MATZOH BREI FOO YONG*

2 matzohs	1-5 oz. can bamboo shoots
1 medium onion sliced	2 nice green scallions
3 tablespoons oil	¾ cup chopped pieces chicken,
4 spoons green pepper	cooked
chopped	4 nice fresh eggs

First break up the matzoh into pieces and soak in water. While this is soaking, sauté the onion in a little oil until it's golden; then add the green pepper for a couple minutes. Now you can throw in also the bamboo shoots, chopped scallions and the chicken. Let cook for 2 more minutes. During this 2 minutes, you can drain the matzoh and add the eggs to it. Don't forget to mix nice. Now you can pour into the matzoh and egg mixture the vegetables and chicken. Mix this all together and fry with a little oil into latkes about the size of a tea saucer.

NOW FOR THE GRAVY:

1 cup water	1 teaspoon MSG
1 tablespoon oil	A pinch pepper
1 teaspoon sugar	2 teaspoons cornstarch
1 teaspoon salt	together with 2 tablespoons
1 teaspoon soy sauce	water

First you should boil the cup water and then add all the other things. Stir for half a minute and pour over each serving. This will make 2 people nice and full and it makes a good change from bagels and lox on Sunday morning.

* MATZOH: that new Jewish diet bread all the goyem are buying.

BEEF LO MEIN BOY CHIK*

¾ pound fresh Chinese noodles
A tablespoon sesame oil
6 pieces tree ear (fungus)
A half cup oil
4 cloves garlic, chopped
½ pound nice steak, shredded
A pinch pepper
A half cup bamboo shoots, shredded

A half cup celery cabbage, shredded
A pinch salt
A pinch sugar
A half cup chicken broth
A tablespoon soy sauce
A half cup coriander leaves (Chinese parsley)

In a big pot water, boil good the noodles for 4 or 5 minutes. When they're ready, you'll drain and rinse in running water. Then you can put them on a flat plate and mix good with the sesame oil. Next, put into boiling water the tree ears and let soak for 15 minutes. Pour the oil in the wok and get good and hot. Put in now the garlic, beef and pepper and cook, stirring nice for about one minute. Now drain off most of the oil and save. Heat the wok up again so you can throw in the bamboo shoots, celery cabbage, salt and sugar. Cook for a minute, you shouldn't forget to stir. Take out from the wok and save. Put in the wok a little of the oil saved from the beef, make hot and throw in the noodles. Stir and cook for about a half minute and then throw in the chicken broth, soy sauce, beef, vegetables and tree ears. Cook this for about 10 minutes while you stir. When you're ready to serve put on top the coriander and you'll have enough for at least 8 people.

* BOY CHIK: A semi-adult male with pimples.

CHICKEN LO MEIN
AHF KAH POO RUSS*

¾ pound Chinese noodles
2 tablespoons sesame oil
6 dried mushrooms
4 tablespoons oil
½ cup chopped scallions

3 cloves garlic chopped
2 cups bean sprouts
A cup cooked and shredded chicken
A pinch salt

A tablespoon light soy

Boil good the noodles in plenty of water for 5 minutes. Then you can drain and rinse off. Spread the noodles on a plate and mix with the sesame oil. Next you should soak the mushrooms in boiling water for 15 minutes and the stems you'll trim off and throw away. In the wok, you'll heat the oil and throw in the scallions and garlic, stir fry for a minute and then throw in the mushrooms, bean sprouts, chicken, salt and soy sauce. Let it cook for a few minutes more and on the noodles you should pour it. Makes enough for 8 persons who don't think about diets.

* *AHF KAH POO RUSS*: Standard and Poor's Financial Rating of New York City.

COLD SESAME NOODLES WITH CHICKEN HAH GAD DAH*

1½ breasts chicken	5 tablespoons light soy
½ lb. Chinese noodles	3 tablespoons wine vinegar
3 tablespoons sesame oil	A little salt
½ cup sesame paste	1 tablespoon sugar
3 tablespoons Hot Oil	⅓ cup oil
3 tablespoons garlic, chopped	

Cook nice the chicken in a pot with 2 quarts water for about 15 minutes or until it's done. Now take out from the water the chicken and put in the noodles. This you'll cook for about 6 to 8 minutes so they are tender. Now drain the noodles and with a little cold water you'll rinse until they get cold. Drain them again and sprinkle on a tablespoon sesame oil, mix it up and let it wait. Meanwhile the sauce you'll make. Put the sesame paste into a bowl and stir it up good with ¼ cup hot water. Now mix in the Hot Oil, soy, wine vinegar, salt, sugar, oil, garlic and the rest of the sesame oil. The noodles now you can put on a serving platter, tear the chicken into little shreds and on top of the noodles you'll put them. On top of this add the sauce and you'll be able to serve 6-8 people. If you have any left over it's nice to eat for a snack during a Johnnie Carson commercial.

* HAH GAD DAH: the only book I'm allowed to read at the table.

38

VEGETABLES

GREEN BEANS HOK MEE
NOH CHY NICK*

½ lb. nice steak
1 tablespoon soy sauce
1 teaspoon MSG
1 teaspoon sugar
1 teaspoon cornstarch

A few pinches salt
A pinch pepper
A little oil
1 package frozen green beans
½ cup water

The steak you'll cut up into small thin pieces (1" x 1" thin). In a bowl you'll put in the soy sauce, MSG, sugar, cornstarch, salt and pepper. Mix this up and put into it the steak, it should stand for a while (10 minutes). Heat the little oil in a frying pan and cook in it the steak for 5 minutes. While it's frying, you should stir. Then you can add the thawed beans, pour in the water and cook it for 15 minutes on a low fire. When it's finished it'll serve 4 people or 2 "nice & healthy" cousins who just dropped in.

* HOK MEE NOH CHY NICK: what Mom says when Irving tries to explain why he was kicked out of Hebrew School.

STRING BEANS TSUR RISS*

1 tablespoon oil
2 cloves garlic
1 medium onion
2 tablespoons soy sauce
1 lb. fresh string beans
1 cup chicken broth

Make hot a frying pan and put in the oil. Slice up the garlic and onion and fry for a while, it should get golden. Then you can add the soy sauce and the string beans, in pieces they should be broken. Pour in now the chicken broth and let the whole thing simmer for 8-10 minutes, or until they're tender, but not so soft there's no vitamins left. This should serve 4 people.

* *TSUR RISS*: when Tillie can't get a beauty parlor appointment in time for the Bar Mitzvah.

EGG PLANT GON IFF*

½ lb. eggplant
4 dried mushrooms soaked
A few slices bamboo shoots
3 or 4 slices nice cooked
  chicken

A pot hot oil for deep-fry
1 tablespoon oil
Meat from 2 or 3 walnuts
A few almonds

SAUCE:

2 tablespoons soy sauce
2 tablespoons sherry
A pinch MSG

First you should peel the eggplant and cut it into wedges, about an inch big they should be. Then you'll cut these wedges into ½ inch pieces. Next the mushrooms, bamboo shoots and chicken you'll slice. Make nice and hot the pot oil and fry in it for 3 minutes the eggplant. Then you'll drain *very, very* well. In a frying pan, put a tablespoon oil and throw in the mushrooms, chicken and bamboo shoots and fry for a minute. Put in the eggplant and the sauce ingredients, and mix nice. Now you can put it on a plate so you can serve. Don't forget to put on top the nuts. This will serve two very hungry people. Sometimes it's nice to fix a little fancy dish even when you're not having company. Your husband will appreciate.

* *GON IFF:* the taxi driver that took you to your hotel in Los Angeles by way of San Diego.

42

CARROTS BUH BUH MY SUH*

5 or 6 nice carrots
1 tablespoon oil
1 cup water
2 tablespoons sugar
A few pinches salt
2 tablespoons vinegar
1 tablespoon cornstarch

Wash nice the carrots and in diagonal slices a half inch thick you'll cut them. Make hot a frying pan and put in the oil. When it's good and hot you'll sauté for a minute the carrots. Then throw in a half cup water. Now you'll cover and boil for 5 minutes until the carrots are soft enough so you can eat. Mix all together the sugar, salt, vinegar, cornstarch and the rest of the water. Put this in the pan with the carrots and let it cook for a little while, it should get thick. This makes a very nice side dish for 4 or 5 people— and it's full with vitamins. You should feed it to the children, it'll put roses in their cheeks.

* *BUH BUH MY SUH:* Richard Nixon exclaiming "I am not a crook!"

SPINACH MISH AH GAHS*

1 lb. fresh spinach
2 tablespoons oil
A few pinches salt
¼ cup chicken broth
1 small can bamboo shoots
8 nice mushrooms

Wash good the spinach, it shouldn't be sandy, and cut it up in 2 inch pieces. Make hot a frying pan and add the oil. When it's good and hot, throw in the salt and the spinach and for two minutes you should fry. Then you can pour in the broth and throw in the bamboo shoots and mushrooms. This you'll cook for a few more minutes and serve right away, it shouldn't get cold.

* MISH AH GAHS: soliciting for the U.J.A. at the Egyptian Embassy.

MIXED VEGETABLES HAH ZAH RYE*

12 shelled almonds
12 chestnuts
 4 tablespoons oil
½ cup diced celery
 6 nice mushrooms
12 water chestnuts in small chunks
 1 cup bean sprouts

1 small can bamboo shoots, sliced
1 cup lettuce
¼ cup soy sauce
A pinch or two salt
2 tablespoons sherry
1 teaspoon cornstarch
3 cups nice fresh chicken broth

In a pot hot water the almonds and chestnuts (*not* the water chestnuts) you should boil for 10 minutes. Then you can take them out from the water and the chestnuts you'll peel. Make hot a large frying pan and put in the oil. Then you should throw in the celery, mushrooms sliced, the water chestnuts, bean sprouts, bamboo shoots, almonds and chestnuts. Let this cook for 5 minutes making sure you stir. Then add in the lettuce, soy sauce, salt, sherry, cornstarch, and chicken broth. Cover the pan and cook on a low fire until all the vegetables are done. Be careful it doesn't cook too much, it shouldn't be mushy. Serve nice and hot with rice.

* *HAH ZAH RYE:* the meat that was taken out from this recipe so it should be Kosher.

THREE COLOR BEAN SPROUTS
TZAH DIK*

½ lb. bean sprouts
8 tree-ear mushrooms (fungus)
2 red chili peppers
2 green peppers
A little oil

A nice pinch salt
A tablespoon chopped ginger
¼ cup nice chicken stock
2 teaspoons light soy
A splash sherry

First you'll blanch in boiling water for a minute or two the bean sprouts. Also, soak for 15 minutes the tree ears in boiling water. When they're soft you'll drain. Clean the peppers and cut them up like matchsticks. Now put a little oil in the wok, put in the salt and ginger and stir fry a little. Next throw in the peppers and tree ears and cook for two minutes more, then add the bean sprouts, stir and pour in the stock, soy and sherry. Put on the cover and let it cook for two minutes more and it's all ready to serve 4 vegetarians.

* *TZAH DIK:* Billy Graham in a yarmulke and talis!

SPICED EGGPLANT MIK VAH*

2 1 lb. eggplants	A tablespoon sherry
A good pinch sugar	A tablespoon sesame oil
3 tablespoons light soy	A tablespoon vegetable oil
2 tablespoons wine vinegar	5 cloves garlic chopped fine
A nice pinch salt	A tablespoon ginger chopped fine

First, in a steamer you'll put the eggplants and cook good
until they look like a flat tire. Let it cool nice while you mix
together the sugar, soy, vinegar, salt, sherry and sesame oil.
Next, a wok you'll make hot and put in the oil so you can
cook for a few seconds the garlic and ginger. Then the
vinegar and soy mish-mash pour in and boil quick for a
minute. While this is getting cool, shred up in pieces the
eggplant and on a nice plate you should put it. Pour over
this the sauce and serve to six people, one of whom insists
that eggplant the Chinese don't have.

* *MIK VAH:* the Orthodox Swim Club.

FAH SHTUNK KEN AH FISH ROLL*

3 nice fresh eggs
1 tablespoon water
2 tablespoons oil
¾ cup chopped flounder (for this is good a blender)
1 tablespoon chopped scallions
2 tablespoons chopped water chestnuts
A little pinch salt
1 tablespoon soy sauce

Put the tablespoon water in the eggs and beat them up. Then make hot a little of the oil in a large frying pan and pour half the eggs in the pan so it covers all over and is thin. Fry it until it's nice and set and then turn it over so you'll cook the other side. Put it aside so it'll cook and fry the rest of the egg mixture the same way. Now you'll mix together the chopped fish, scallions, water chestnuts, salt and soy sauce. Put half of it on one of the egg pieces and smooth it out nice, it should cover all over. Then you can roll it up like a piece strudel, put some flour on the edges and press the edges together so they don't come apart. Do the same thing with the other piece egg. Cut the rolls up with a sharp knife (you shouldn't cut yourself) in ¼ inch slices. Make hot in the frying pan the rest of the oil and fry the slices so they'll be a nice golden brown. This makes enough for 6 people.

SAUCE:

1½ tablespoons soy sauce
¾ cup water
1 tablespoon cornstarch
½ teaspoon sugar

Mix together the soy sauce and cornstarch so it should be smooth. Add the water and sugar and for 5 minutes you'll boil. Pour on the slices and serve.

* FAH SHTUNK KEN AH: even his best friends won't tell him!

HADDOCK YEN TAH*

6 mushrooms
1 lb. haddock filet
1 tablespoon cornstarch
2 tablespoons oil
1 fat clove garlic minced
2 nice scallions
½ can bamboo shoots
1 tablespoon vinegar
4 tablespoons sherry
A few pinches salt

First you'll take the mushrooms and cut them in chunks. Now, the fish you'll cut into pieces about an inch or two square and sprinkle on the cornstarch all over. Then in a frying pan you'll heat the oil and put in the garlic and fry for a minute. Next put in the fish and sauté for 2 or 3 minutes more. Take out the fish from the pan and put aside for a while. Add to the pan the scallions chopped, the bamboo shoots, the mushrooms, the vinegar, sherry and salt. Cook this for a couple minutes, you shouldn't forget to stir. Now you can add a half teaspoon cornstarch mixed in with a little water and then the fish and cook for about 2 or 3 minutes. If your neighbor comes to your door to ask what smells, invite the Yen Tah in for dinner.

* YEN TAH: a free-lance social worker.

FISH NEH BISH*

1½ lbs. filet of sole	2 tablespoons oil
2 scallions	2 nice fresh eggs
2 tablespoons soy sauce	2 teaspoons cornstarch
1 tablespoon sherry	A pinch sugar
A few pinches salt	3 tablespoons water
1 small can pineapple chunks	

First you'll take a knife and cut up each piece fish across in strips an inch wide. Then chop up the scallions and with the soy sauce, sherry and salt, you'll mix. Put in this the pieces fish and soak for a few minutes. Now you'll heat up the oil in a frying pan. While it heats, beat up the eggs and mix in the cornstarch. In this, the fish you'll dip. Then you can fry the pieces fish for a couple minutes on each side so it's cooked. When it's ready, you'll drain and put on a serving dish. Next the sugar and water you'll add to the leftover dipping mixture, also the pineapple chunks. Put this into the pan and cook for a few minutes until it gets thick and almost clear looking. Now you can pour it on the fish and it's ready to serve about 4 people.

* NEH BISH: a man who asks the Chinese waiter if he can sub-stitute french frys for rice.

HALIBUT CANTONESE
LANTZ MAHN*

1½ lbs. halibut in small chunks	1 chopped onion
1 tablespoon oil	1 sliced scallion
2 mashed cloves garlic	1 tablespoon chopped celery
	1 nice fresh egg

Put the halibut in a pot water and boil for 2 minutes. Then you can put in a frying pan the oil and brown the onions. When they're nice and brown, put in the chunks fish.

SAUCE:

1½ cups water	1 teaspoon MSG
1 tablespoon oil	A pinch pepper
A few pinches salt	2 tablespoons cornstarch in 3 tablespoons water
3 teaspoons soy sauce	

Mix together the stuff for the sauce, but not the cornstarch. Pour this on the fish together with the garlic, scallions and celery. Put on the pan a cover and you'll simmer for 2 minutes. Now beat up nice the egg and pour slow into the sauce. Keep mixing while you pour. After this, you should pour in the cornstarch mixture and stir it up good. Let this whole thing cook until it gets thick.

* CANTONESE LANTZ MAHN: that's funny; you don't *look* Jewish!

HALIBUT SHREDS GON
TZE MAH KER*

2 tablespoons oil	¼ cup soy sauce
1 lb. flaked halibut	¼ cup sherry
¼ teaspoon ginger powder	A few pinches sugar
4 nice scallions sliced	

Heat up in the frying pan a little oil and fry the fish flakes and ginger for a couple minutes. Then throw in the soy sauce, sherry, sugar and the sliced scallions. Let this cook on a low fire and don't forget to stir. This will be ready when most of the juice disappears. 4 nice servings this should make.

* GON TZE MAH KER: the Uncle Sol in everyone's family, who says don't do anything 'til you call me first.

FISH CAKE SHA LOM*

1½ lbs. flounder filet	1 tablespoon soy sauce
1 cup blanched almonds	1 tablespoon cornstarch
A few pinches salt	in a little water
2 sliced scallions	¾ cup oil

Chop up nice the fish (in a blender it's easier) and the almonds. Then you can mix in the scallions, salt, soy sauce, cornstarch mixture and 1½ tablespoons oil. This you can pat into nice flat latkes, about 2 tablespoons to a latke. Make hot the rest of the oil in the frying pan and fry for a few minutes until they get brown on both sides. This will make enough for 5 or 6 people, they should live and be well.

* SHA LOM: Stanley's first word to Dr. Livingston.

FISH BAH LAH BOO STAH*

1 nice 2 lb. carp
¼ cup oil
½ teaspoon powdered ginger
3 nice sliced scallions
3 cloves garlic chopped
A few pinches salt
½ cup sliced mushrooms
1 tablespoon sherry
3 tablespoons soy sauce
1 cup vegetable stock
A pinch sugar
½ teaspoon anise seed

Leave whole the fish but clean it nice and then dry it. Next you can make a few cuts with a knife on each side. Put in the oil in a frying pan and get it good and hot. Fry the fish for a little while, it should get nice and brown. On both sides you shouldn't forget to do this. Then pour off some of the oil and add the ginger, scallions, garlic, salt, mushrooms, sherry, soy sauce, stock, sugar and anise seed. Cover the pan and cook on a low fire for 30 minutes. Maybe you should also turn the fish once in a while so it should cook nice. This will serve 4 people, if you serve also a few other things.

* BAH LAH BOO STAH: someone who cleans her house before the maid comes, she shouldn't find it dirty.

55

TUNA LUCK SHEN
GRO SING GUHS*

2 tablespoons oil
1 sliced onion
1 cup bean sprouts
1 small can bamboo shoots
1 can mushrooms
A little green pepper
  chopped

A little chopped celery
1 cup vegetable stock
¼ cup soy sauce
2 cans tuna fish (7 oz. each)
A box thin noodles (12 oz.)
1 tablespoon cornstarch
4 tablespoons water

Heat the oil in a frying pan and cook in it the onions for a few minutes. Then you'll put in all the vegetables, stock, soy sauce and the tuna fish. This you should cover and cook maybe 12 minutes.

While this is on the stove, you'll cook the noodles like the box says.

After the tuna mish-mash has cooked for 12 minutes, mix the cornstarch with the water and pour it in. In a minute the whole thing will get a little thick. Then it's ready to mix with the noodles. This should be for 6 people, they should live and be well.

* *GRO SING GUHS*: the East Coast matrimonial bureau for teen-age spinsters.

BRAISED FISH GAH NU VIM*

A nice 2 lb. fish, whole and cleaned
A little salt and pepper
A little flour for dredging
6 tablespoons oil
4 dried mushrooms, soaked and sliced

2 scallions, chopped
½ cup bamboo shoots, sliced
3 nice slices ginger
A cup fish stock
3 tablespoons light soy
A nice pinch salt
A pinch sugar

On the fish you'll sprinkle a little salt and pepper and flour it nice. In a pan you'll make hot the oil and put in the fish for one minute on each side. Also baste a little with the hot oil while you're frying. Lower the fire and cook for a few minutes more and then throw on the mushrooms, scallions, bamboo shoots, ginger, stock, soy, salt and sugar. Put on a cover and cook over a medium fire for about 15 minutes but the fish you should turn gently once while it cooks. Feeds about 4 people either hot or cold (the fish, not the people).

* *GAH NU VIM:* Yiddish term meaning "politicians".

STEAMED FISH LIT VAK*

A 1½ lb. flounder, whole but cleaned	2 tablespoons chopped ginger
A little oil	2 scallions, chopped
4 cloves garlic, chopped fine	A tablespoon light soy
	2 teaspoons sugar

3 tablespoons bean sauce

The fish you'll put on a pan and into a boiling steamer for about 15 minutes. While you're steaming, you can also make hot the oil in a wok and throw in the rest of the ingredients and cook for a minute or so. When it's done, the fish, pour off from the pan the liquid and throw away. Now you can pour on the sauce from the wok and serve to 3 or 4 people who never had a piece flounder like this.

* *LIT VAK:* an underprivileged Galitzianer.

SZECHUAN FISH YACH NAH*

4 dried mushrooms, soaked
2 tablespoons chopped bamboo
   shoots
1 hot green pepper, chopped
2 chopped scallions
1 tablespoon chopped ginger
1 lb. fish filets in 2" squares
A little salt and pepper
Flour for dredging
An egg
3 tablespoons sherry
5 tablespoons flour

Oil to deep fry
A little more oil
3 tablespoons light soy
A good pinch chili pepper
A splash sherry
1 tablespoon black soy
1 cup stock
½ teaspoon chili paste with
   garlic
1 tablespoon corn starch
2 tablesoons water
A pinch sugar

Mix together the mushrooms, bamboo shoots, pepper, scallions and ginger. Salt and pepper the fish and in the flour you'll dredge. Now mix up the egg, sherry and flour and make a nice batter. Dip in each piece of fish and deep fry a few at a time until they're nice and golden. Take out from the oil and drain. Now put a little oil in a wok and stir fry the chopped vegetables for a few minutes together with the light soy, chili pepper, sherry, black soy. Then you can put in the stock, chili paste and the pieces fish. Let this whole thing simmer for 5 minutes. Mix together the cornstarch and water and when everything looks ready stir it in so you'll get a little thick. Now stir in the sugar and it's all ready. This serves 6 fish lovers.

* YACH NAH: A Yentah with an audience of other yentahs.

59

FOWL

PINEAPPLE CHICKEN FAY
GEL LAH*

2 nice egg yolks	1 pot hot oil
⅔ cup water	1 teaspoon cornstarch
3 tablespoons flour	¼ cup nice chicken broth
A pinch salt	½ teaspoon powdered ginger
1 teaspoon soy sauce	½ cup pineapple juice
1½ cups cooked chicken in bite–size pieces	1 cup chunks canned pineapple

Mix together nice the egg yolks, water, flour, salt and half the soy sauce. Now you'll dip in the pieces chicken and fry it in the oil until it's good and brown. Next mix together the cornstarch, chicken broth, ginger, the rest of the soy sauce and the pineapple juice. Put this in a pot and you'll boil until it gets thick. Put in the pineapple chunks, and on the chicken pieces you'll pour. Serve it nice and hot with rice, for 6 people. This dish, believe me, they'll love on Fire Island.

* FAY GEL LAH: "my son, the dancer."

62

CHICKEN GAH BAR DEEN*

4 lbs. nice roasting chicken	2 chopped cloves garlic
¼ cup soy sauce	8 dried mushrooms
3 tablespoons sherry	2 tablespoons oil
A few pinches salt	1 cup nice chicken broth
A little pinch pepper	1½ tablespoons cornstarch
½ teaspoon powdered ginger	A pinch sugar

Wash and dry nice the chicken and mix together 3 table-spoons soy sauce, salt, sherry, pepper, ginger and garlic. Rub good into the chicken and soak for an hour. Now soak the mushrooms for 30 minutes and then cut into nice slices. Next make hot the oil in a casserole and brown in it the chicken. Now you can throw in the mushrooms and ¾ of the broth and cook on a low fire for a half hour, it should be tender. When it's done, take out from the pot the chicken and you'll chop yourself up in little bite-size pieces. Next you'll mix the cornstarch with the rest of the broth and the rest of the soy sauce and the sugar. Put this in the casserole with the juice that's there already and keep stirring it until it boils and gets good and thick. Now you can throw in the pieces chicken and cook for a little while longer until it's all hot. This will serve 4 "piece goods" salesmen.

* GAH BAR DEEN: what Bar Mitzvah suits used to be made of.

VELVET CHICKEN MEH GILL LAH*

8 ounces of chicken breast	3 teaspoons cornstarch mixed
1 cup nice chicken broth	in a little water
2 teaspoons salt	8 egg whites
2 teaspoons sherry	A pot oil so you can deep fry
1 teaspoon MSG	

Remove the meat from the bone and mince it up nice and fine. (This is very important; make sure it should be a creamy paste. A blender for this is perfect.) Add to this 6 tablespoons of the chicken broth and mix it up good. Then you should add the salt, sherry and half the cornstarch mixture to the egg whites and with the chicken mix it. Now in a pot of good hot oil, you'll pour in some of the mixture and let it cook for 10-15 seconds. Then stir the oil a little underneath (be careful you shouldn't touch the chicken) so you'll help it rise to the top. When it finally rises, you can turn it over so the other side should also cook. When it gets a nice golden brown take it out from the oil and start all over until all the stuff is used up. Put them on paper, they should drain; and then put in a dish so you can serve. Next take the rest of the broth, cornstarch and MSG and heat it up. When it gets good and thick, pour it over the chicken and serve. This should be enough for 4 people and maybe one of them will be able to give you an idea on how to use up 8 leftover egg yolks.

* MEH GILL LAH: a Jewish Federal case.

CELESTIAL CHICKEN IN
SILVER PACKAGE OH
REE YEN TAH*

2 nice chicken breasts
3 tablespoons soy sauce
1 tablespoon oil
½ cup mushrooms chopped
A pinch ginger

4 tablespoons chopped scallions
1 tablespoon chopped water chestnuts
1 tablespoon sherry

A pot hot oil so you can fry

Take from the breasts chicken, the skin and bones. With a mallet, pound flat the pieces chicken and cut into 2 inch squares. Sprinkle on a little soy sauce and let stand for a few minutes. While it's standing, heat a little oil in a pan and sauté the vegetables for a few minutes. Then pour in the rest of the soy sauce, ginger and sherry. Let it cool and then spread a little bit on each piece chicken. Fold over the chicken squares (like little envelopes they should be) and wrap also like an envelope in a piece aluminum foil (3 or 4 inches square). When they are all made and wrapped, let them cool for a while and then deep fry them for about 4 minutes in the hot oil (375°). Makes 10-12 pieces. When the neighbors smell this cooking, they'll think you've gone "trafe"—but you shouldn't worry. The Rabbi says it's Kosher, so who cares from the neighbors?

* OH REE YEN TAH: a lady Chinese gossip.

CHICKEN GOY YIM*

1 lb. chicken breasts	1 scallion
3 cups boiling water	½ teaspoon pepper

SAUCE:

2 tablespoons sherry	1 teaspoon sugar
2 tablespoons oil	¼ teaspoon vinegar
5 tablespoons soy sauce	

Cover the chicken with hot boiling water and for 10-12 minutes it should cook. While it's cooking you can mix up the sauce and heat. Chop up in pieces the scallion. When the chicken finishes cooking you'll take a cleaver (watch out you shouldn't cut the fingers) and cut the breasts crosswise right through the bone in pieces ¾ of an inch wide. This you can put on a serving dish, sprinkle on the chopped scallions and pepper. Also, the sauce you shouldn't forget to pour on. This will serve 2 people, but also make lots of tea. For salt-free diets, this isn't.

* GOY YIM: what some of our best friends are.

CHICKEN PIPP ICK*

2 tablespoons oil	4 stalks celery in thin pieces
3 lb. fryer chopped in pieces, bite–size	2 nice handfuls spinach
	4 scallions
2 cups chopped water chestnuts	2 cups bamboo shoots
	A tiny pinch ginger
2 cups chopped mushrooms	1 cup nice chicken broth

1 large onion sliced

SAUCE:

2 tablespoons cornstarch	A little pinch pepper
3 teaspoons soy sauce	A little pinch sugar
A pinch salt	A pinch MSG

4 tablespoons water

Make hot the oil in a pot and brown in it the chicken. Then add all the vegetables, the ginger and the broth and simmer for twenty minutes. Next blend the sauce ingredients together and add to the mixture and stir until it gets nice and thick. This serves about 5 people, they should live to be a hundred and twenty.

---

* *PIPP ICK:* the first part of his anatomy a baby discovers.

67

CHICKEN WALNUT AH MENCH*

1 medium size chicken	½ cup chopped celery
3 tablespoons soy sauce	6 water chestnuts sliced
2 tablespoons sherry	½ cup bamboo shoots
1 tablespoon cornstarch	1 medium onion sliced
1 cup walnuts shelled	½ cup bean sprouts
6 tablespoons oil	A pinch salt
½ cup sliced mushrooms	¼ cup nice chicken broth

Take from the chicken all the meat and cut into ½ inch pieces. Mix together the soy sauce, sherry, and cornstarch and soak in it the meat. Blanch the walnuts and fry in 2 tablespoons oil so they get brown. Then you should drain. Now you'll take a hot frying pan and put in 2 tablespoons oil. In this you'll put all the vegetables and salt and sauté until they are about half done. Now you'll take out and put aside. Put 2 more tablespoons oil in the pan and put in the pieces chicken. This you'll fry for a few minutes until it's cooked. When it's ready, you'll put back the vegetables and on this pour in the broth and put in the walnuts. Heat for another 2 minutes and it's ready to serve.

* *AH MENCH:* Uncle Leon, the lawyer; he has his own office.

CHICKEN LUCK SHEN
DAH REE ANN*

¼ lb. nice, rich egg noodles
1 tablespoon oil
A pinch salt
1 cup sliced Chinese celery
   cabbage, (or American
   celery)
½ cup bean sprouts

A few nice mushrooms
¼ lb. cooked, diced chicken
¼ cup water
1 tablespoon soy sauce
1 teaspoon MSG
A pinch sugar
A little pepper

In a pot with 2 quarts boiling water you should cook the noodles for 8 minutes and then drain. Next heat a frying pan with a little oil on a high fire. Add the salt, celery cabbage, bean sprouts, mushrooms and chicken. Keep mixing while you fry it for 2 or 3 minutes. After this, pour in the water and the noodles, they should be on top. Cover the pan and cook for about 2 to 3 minutes. Now you can mix in the soy sauce, MSG, sugar and pepper. Cook for another minute and you're all done. It's a very good way to use up the leftovers from Friday night's boiled chicken.

* DAH REE ANN: proposed site of the first Jewish sit-in.

69

HONEY CHICKEN NOF KAH*

A nice young fryer
4 tablespoons oil
A walnut-sized piece ginger,
   sliced

2 tablespoons honey
A good splash sherry
A good splash black soy
A pinch salt

First you'll cut good the chicken into bite-size pieces. In the wok, put the oil and the ginger and into this you should put the chicken. Stir fry this until the chicken, it's good and brown. Now, you can pour off the extra oil and the honey, sherry, soy sauce and salt you'll put in. Make low the fire, put on a cover and you'll cook for about 30 minutes. There will be enough, maybe for six people.

* NOF KAH: She doesn't type or take shorthand but to the Senator she's indispensable!

70

SZECHUAN SPICY CHICKEN
MET TZE AH*

2 nice breasts chicken, boned	A teaspoon sugar
1 egg white beaten up	A pinch MSG
A tablespoon cornstarch	A little sherry
A pinch salt	A tablespoon vinegar
A tablespoon bean sauce	5 cloves chopped garlic
A tablespoon Hoi Sin sauce	6 red hot dried peppers
A teaspoon chili paste with garlic	A cup oil

Cut up good the chicken into bite sizes and mix with the
egg white, cornstarch and salt. This you'll let stand in the
ice box for a half hour. While you're waiting, mix together
the bean sauce, Hoi Sin sauce, chili paste, sugar, MSG,
sherry, vinegar and garlic. Now, put in the wok the oil and
when it's good and hot throw in the chicken and you'll
cook for about a minute, stirring good. Take out from the
wok the chicken and pour off most of the oil, leaving just
a little bit. Put in now the peppers and cook them for about
30 seconds, then throw in the chicken and the sauce mish-
mash and let cook for another minute or two so the chicken
should cook and the sauce mix nice. This makes enough
for 6 people, they couldn't have ulcers.

* *MET TZE AH:* What good garage sales are made of.

CORIANDER CHICKEN SHREDS
TCHEP PAH*

A nice chicken, already cooked
1 teaspoon powdered mustard
2 teaspoons light soy
1 cup coriander (Chinese parsley)
6 scallions, chopped
A little salt
A pinch sugar

Take off from the bones, the chicken meat and tear into little pieces. Now mix up the mustard with 2 teaspoons boiling water and blend it in with the chicken. Next you can throw in the soy, most of the coriander, scallions, salt and sugar. Put this on a serving plate and decorate a little with the left over coriander and you'll have enough for 6 people who need a low-calorie snack.

TCHEP PAH: What Mom does when you haven't called for two days.

TURKEY CHOW MEIN HUTZ PAH*

2 tablespoons oil
2 nice onions sliced
2 cups sliced celery
¾ lb. sliced mushrooms
1½ cups nice chicken broth
1 small can water chestnuts
1 cup bean sprouts

1 small can bamboo shoots
3 tablespoons soy sauce
1 tablespoon cornstarch
3 cups shredded cooked
   turkey
A package crisp Chinese
   noodles

Make hot in a frying pan the oil and fry the onions until they get tender. Then add the celery, mushrooms and broth and for 5 minutes you'll cook. Throw in the water chestnuts, bean sprouts and bamboo shoots and cook for a few minutes more. Now mix together the soy sauce and the cornstarch and throw also into the pan. Keep on cooking and stirring until it gets nice and thick. Now you can put in the turkey and cook for a few minutes more, it should get hot. When it's all ready, you'll pour it on the noodles and serve right away, it mustn't get cold. Believe me, this is the best way to finish up from Thanksgiving.

* HUTZ PAH: describes anyone who asks a bus driver, at the rush hour, if he has change of $5.

ROAST DUCK FAH BRENT*

A nice 5 lb. duck
4 teaspoons honey
¼ cup chicken broth
4 teaspoons sugar
1 tablespoon soy sauce
A pinch salt

Mix together everything but the duck. In this mixture you'll soak for an hour the duck. Then on a rack in a roasting pan with a little water in the bottom, put the bird. Place this in a 350° oven for 2 hours. Every once in a while you should baste a little. For the last 10 minutes, turn up the oven to high so the duck gets nice and crisp and brown. When it's all done, cut the duck into pieces and serve with duck sauce. About 4 people should make a meal from this.

If you're among friends, serve toothpicks after this. (The pretty colored ones are nice for a festive touch.)

* FAH BRENT: what happens to the food in the oven when the timer breaks down and Mom's been on the phone who knows how long!

74

ROAST DUCK QVEH CHING*

A nice 5 lb. duck
1 cup soy sauce
2 tablespoons powdered ginger
A little oil

Clean good the duck and take out as much fat as you can.
Then mix together in a pot the soy sauce, ginger, the duck
and enough water so you'll cover. Now you'll boil for an
hour on a low flame. When it's ready, take out the duck and
throw away the liquid. With a little oil you should brush
the duck all over and put it on a rack in a roasting pan.
Roast it in the oven at 425° for 45 minutes until the duck
is tender. Then you'll turn up the oven to high for 5
minutes so the skin should get nice and crisp. This should
serve 4 people.

* QVEH CHING: when you ask someone how he feels and he
tells you.

VUS MAHKS DOO DUCKLING*

1-4 lb. duckling	1 green pepper in pieces
2 tablespoons oil	A few chopped scallions
A pinch salt	2 tablespoons cornstarch
A pinch pepper	2 teaspoons soy sauce
1 small can pineapple chunks	¼ cup water

In boiling water cover the duck and cook for 45 minutes, it should be tender. Take out the duck and save the broth. (If you let it boil by itself for a while it'll be richer.) Put in a large frying pan the oil, salt and pepper and get it hot. In the meanwhile, you can cut the duck into serving pieces and when the oil is hot you'll fry for a while, it should get brown all over. Then you'll add 1½ cups of the duck broth skimmed, the pineapple chunks and the green pepper. For 10 minutes this should cook. Near the end you can throw in the scallions. While it's still cooking at the end of the 10 minutes, you'll mix together the cornstarch, soy sauce and water and this you'll also throw in. Let it cook for a few minutes more so it thickens and it's nice and hot. Serve it right away with rice. It's enough for 4 people, and a nice change from Friday night boiled chicken.

* VUS MAHKS DOO? the first telegraph message ever sent.

76

GINGER DUCK HOO HA*

A nice duck
A scallion, chopped up
A tablespoon cornstarch
2 tablespoons light soy

A tablespoon sherry
A nice pinch salt
A little oil
3 tablespoons chopped ginger

Take off first from the duck all the meat. (The frame you should save for soup.) Now you'll mix the scallion, cornstarch, soy sauce, sherry and salt. Next, you'll throw in the duck and do something else for a half hour or so. When you're ready make hot in the wok the oil and put the duck mish-mash in and stir fry for a couple minutes. When it looks half done, the ginger you'll throw in and cook for 3 minutes more, while you're still stirring. Makes enough for 4 people or 2 fressers.

* *HOO HA:* The Hee Haw re-runs renamed for Israeli TV.

SPICY FRIED DUCK SHMA TAH*

2 sticks cinnamon, cracked and broken

2 tablespoons salt

3 nice pieces star anise

1 big teaspoon Szechuan peppercorns

A nice duck

A good chunk ginger

A few scallions

Some flour

2 tablespoons black soy

4 tablespoons cornstarch

1 tablespoon sherry (should be dry)

2 egg whites

A pinch sugar

Enough oil so you can fry

Mix first together the cinnamon, salt, star anise and peppercorns. But make sure it's broken up good the cinnamon and star anise. Now you'll rub all over the duck like a good massage and stick inside the ginger and scallions. The taste will be better if you keep in the ice box all night. When you're ready to cook rub all over some flour and in a steamer you'll steam for an hour and a half. After you're finished steaming you'll cool off for a while and rub on good the soy sauce. Now, the duck you can put in the ice box if you want to take a nap or whatever. When the dinner you're ready for, you can mix up good the egg whites, sherry, sugar and cornstarch and a paste you'll make. Shmear this nice over the duck and for a half hour it should wait. Enough oil you should put in a wok so the duck will be half in and half out. Turn on the fire and make hot the oil. Carefully the duck you'll put in and let fry. While you're frying you should also with a big spoon spill hot oil on the top of the duck. When a nice golden tan the bottom

* *SHMA TAH:* Last year's mink.

78

gets, turn over and on the other side you'll do the same. When it gets crisp and brown like two weeks in Puerto Rico you're done. Take out from the oil, drain nice and you'll qvell when you serve it. There will be enough for six people who don't like duck but "this is different"!

You should bite your tongue!

PORK

BEEF FLON KEN SWEET AND SOUR*

½ lb. nice lean beef   1 teaspoon cornstarch
2 tablespoons soy sauce   3 tablespoons oil
8 or 10 radishes

SAUCE:

1 tablespoon cornstarch
⅓ cup vinegar   ⅓cup sugar

First you'll slice very thin the beef and you'll mix together the soy sauce and cornstarch. Smear all over the beef slices with this mixture. In a frying pan, you'll put 2 tablespoons oil and begin to heat it. When it's hot, it's time to put in the vinegar, sugar and cornstarch, you shouldn't forget to mix. Then you can throw in the beef slices and let them cook until they get just a teeny bit brown. When that happens, you can add the radishes sliced and cook just long enough so they get hot. If you cook longer, they won't be crisp; they'll be, as said in Chinese, "Vee ah shmah tah." Serve it right away with other dishes so no one should get hungry. We can't tell you how many persons this serves unless we know what else you're serving with it.

* FLON KEN: you were expecting maybe porterhouse?

BEEF SHIK SUH WITH CAULIFLOWER*

¾ lb. lean beef
2 tablespoons oil
1 small onion chopped
2 cloves garlic minced
1 cup beef broth

1 small head cauliflower
1 lb. shelled peas
½ cup bean sprouts
½ cup mushrooms
½ cup bamboo shoots

A few pinches salt

SAUCE:

2 tablespoons cornstarch
3 teaspoons soy sauce

½ cup water
2 teaspoons sherry

Slice thin the beef. Into the frying pan put the oil and get it good and hot; then add the beef, garlic, onion and cook until the meat gets nice and brown. Then pour in the beef broth and the cauliflower broken into 'flowerlets' and the rest of the vegetables and the salt. Cover it up; make a low fire and cook for about 15 minutes. While it's cooking, mix together the cornstarch, soy sauce, water and sherry. Then after the 15 minutes, pour this mixture in and cook until it gets thick. Serves about 3 or 4 people. If the grandchildren are coming for dinner, have chopsticks at the table at least. But have plenty napkins also.

* SHIK SUH: Any girl with blonde hair. If she also has blue eyes, she's a "Regular shik suh".

BLUSHING BEEF SHLUH MEEL*

½ lb. steak	A few pinches salt
A little oil	4 tablespoons water
4 tomatoes	1 teaspoon soy sauce
1 tablespoon cornstarch	A pinch or two sugar

Slice the meat into very thin slices almost like paper. Then make hot the oil and fry the meat very quickly. Take out from the pan the meat, skin the tomatoes and put them in to warm up a little. While it's warming, you can mix together the cornstarch, salt, water, soy sauce and sugar. Then put the meat back with the tomatoes and add the mixture. Heat it until it's thick. It should serve from 4 to 5 people, if you are also serving other things, and maybe you should.

* SHLUH MEEL: he asks a P.L.O. official to speak at a Bonds for Israel rally.

MEAT THREADS KUPP DRAY
NISH WITH VEGETABLES*

2 teaspoons oil	1 cup sliced water chestnuts
2 medium onions chopped	1 cup bean sprouts
1½ cups chicken broth	5 leaves Chinese celery (or
2 tablespoons soy sauce	American celery)
1 lb. steak cut into *thin* strips	4 scallions chopped
1 cup sliced mushrooms	1 teaspoon sugar
1 cup bamboo shoots	A few pieces watercress

1 teaspoon MSG

Heat very hot the oil and sauté the onions. Then add some of the broth and soy sauce and stir for a few minutes. Add the rest of the ingredients except the MSG and cook for 15 minutes. Turn off the heat and add the MSG. Mix it up good and serve it with rice or some nice kasha. Serves 3. This you make a mistake if you don't serve with *fleischa-dik* chopsticks.

* *KUPP DRAY NISH*: this you have when the wedding is cancelled after the gifts have started arriving.

87

BEEF FON DOO*

For this you'll need a half pound steak each. Then you should cut up the steak into pieces just big enough for a good bite.

On the table you'll put a chafing dish with a pot full of hot oil.

Everybody should have a long fork. Stick it into the piece meat and put into the hot oil. Leave it for a minute or so and when it comes out . . . oh boy!

Then you can dip it into duck sauce and hot mustard or even the applesauce with horseradish. This is so exotic you shouldn't know from it.

(So your guests shouldn't go hungry, be sure to serve other things with this, like maybe vegetables, rice . . . the usual . . . but try candlelight . . . that, with the flame from the chafing dish . . . such ooh's and aah's you'll get from the family!)

---

* FON DOO: this is not a Jewish word . . . it's Swiss. But it's all right, you shouldn't worry . . . with the Swiss we never had any tsurris.

SAH DRAY TAH BEEF*

2 tablespoons oil

A pinch or two salt

A pinch pepper

1 lb. nice steak sliced thin

2 diced up onions

2 cloves garlic

1 cup chicken or beef broth

A few mushrooms sliced

2 green peppers diced

4 red tomatoes small, chunks

2 tablespoons cornstarch

2 teaspoons soy sauce

¼ cup water

In a hot frying pan you'll put the oil and salt and pepper. In this you should fry the slices steak together with the onion and garlic. When it gets brown the steak, you can add already the cup of broth and the diced green peppers and mushrooms. This you'll cook for about 10 minutes with the cover on. Then you'll throw in the tomato chunks and cook for another minute. While it's cooking, you'll hurry up and mix together the cornstarch, soy sauce and water. Throw this in the pan and cook until it gets thick and the whole thing is good and hot. This you should serve with boiled rice. It's enough for 4 people.

* SAH DRAY TAH: a baseball player who wants to play in the Arab League.

BEEF GOY ISH AH KUPP*

1 lb. nice steak	¼ teaspoon ginger
3 tablespoons oil	2 tablespoons soy sauce
2 big onions	1 teaspoon MSG
3 cloves garlic	A pinch or two salt
1 lb. mushrooms	A little pepper
1 cup chicken broth	3 teaspoons cornstarch

First you should cut the steak into very thin slices about ⅛ inch thick and about 2 inches long. (Exact you don't have to be, nobody will measure.) Then put 2 tablespoons oil into a frying pan and make it good and hot. Into this put the steak slices and fry it until it gets brown. You'll also find a little juice in the pan after this, so take out from the pan the steak and the juice, and put on the side for a while. Then put the other spoon oil into the pan and fry the onions, you shouldn't forget to slice, and the garlic. When this is soft and golden you can throw in the sliced mushrooms and cook for a little while more. Then you should put back the steak slices and juice, and put in the chicken broth, ginger, soy sauce, MSG, salt and pepper. Let this cook for about 3 minutes. Add the cornstarch, first mixed with a little water and cook 2 minutes more. Serve with rice to about 3 or 4 people.

* GOY ISH AH KUPP: refers to anyone who pays a retail price when he can get it wholesale.

SWEET AND PUNGENT BEEF CHUNKS OY GAH VALT*

1½ lbs. steak
2 fresh eggs
1 crushed garlic clove
¾ cup cornstarch
A pot hot oil
1 No. 2 can chunks pineapple

¾ cup white vinegar
A few pinches salt
½ cup sugar
2 cups water
2 green peppers cut into pieces
2 nice tomatoes in pieces

The steak you'll cut into one inch pieces. Then beat up the eggs and the piece garlic together and dip in the beef. Then, in a half cup cornstarch you'll roll around the beef, and then put them into the hot oil and cook until it's brown. Then you'll put them on paper, they should drain. Take from the can pineapple the juice, and mix it with the rest of the cornstarch. Then mix in the vinegar, salt, sugar and water. Cook this on a low fire for a few minutes until it's nice and thick. Then throw in the pineapple, the green peppers, the tomatoes and the beef chunks. Keep cooking for about 5 minutes and it's ready to serve about 6 people. (This even the daughter-in-law will really enjoy.)

* OY GAH VALT: what you say on Yuntif in synagogue when the lady in front of you is wearing the same hat you are!

PEPPER STEAK SHAY
NUH KIN DUH*

4 tablespoons oil	1 clove minced garlic
1 lb. steak in little pieces	1 chopped scallion
A pinch pepper	1 cup chicken broth
A few pinches salt	1 tablespoon soy sauce
3 nice size peppers	4 tablespoons water
2 tablespoons cornstarch	

First you should brown the meat in a little oil and then sprinkle on the salt and pepper. Then you can add the peppers, garlic and scallion. On this, pour the chicken broth and cover and cook for ten minutes. Now you can mix together the soy sauce; water and cornstarch also add. Cook for a few more minutes until it gets thick and it's ready to serve about 4 people. It's also nice to put a little rice on the table, or maybe even some noodles. If those stubborn kids couldn't make it for dinner, you should freeze the leftovers. Or better yet, it won't kill you to eat it for 2 days.

* *SHAY NUH KIN DUH*: those kids from next door who put their feet on the new sofa.

92

BEEF WITH GINGER
PAY YESS*

1 lb. nice steak
1 tablespoon black soy
2 tablespoons cornstarch
A pinch salt
A little sugar
½ cup shredded ginger
A splash sherry
A little pinch MSG
2 cups coriander (Chinese parsley)
2 tablespoons oil

Cut first the beef into shreds. (It's better you should freeze a little first.) Now mix up good in a bowl the beef with the soy sauce and cornstarch and let stand for 15 minutes. In a hot wok, you'll put the oil and cook quickly the beef until it's not raw looking anymore. Take out from the wok and stir fry the ginger for a minute or two. Now you'll put back the beef and throw in the salt, sugar, sherry and MSG. Cook for a minute and then you'll add the coriander for a few seconds. You'll have enough for 4-6 people, depending how hungry.

* *PAY YESS:* Stanley's mother qvelled when he grew these. She didn't know he was joining an "acid rock" band.

HOT BEEF SHREDS
GREP SAH LA*

A nice piece steak, 2 lbs.	3 green peppers, the hot kind,
2 tablespoons black soy	chopped
1 tablespoon cornstarch	Another tablespoon black soy
A little oil	A pinch MSG
4 pieces garlic chopped	A pinch salt
1 tablespoon shredded ginger	Maybe a little water

3 scallions chopped

Cut first the steak into pieces like matchsticks. If you freeze a little first it's easier. Now you'll mix up the soy sauce and cornstarch and let sit for a half hour. When you're ready, put a little oil in the wok and you'll throw in the garlic and ginger. Stir it good and then put in the meat. Keep on stirring for a minute or two and then the hot peppers you'll put in. Also, don't forget the tablespoon soy, MSG, salt and a little water if you need. When it's cooked, you'll know, but be careful, it cooks fast. Throw on now the scallions and you're ready to serve 6 people with iron stomachs, it's so spicy.

* GREP SAH LA: This is to seltzer what a hangover is to a martini.

CUCUMBER VEAL MEES KITE*

½ lb. veal	1 tablespoon oil
2 teaspoons cornstarch	4 nice mushrooms sliced
A pinch salt	1 nice peeled cucumber in
2 teaspoons water	small chunks
3 teaspoons soy sauce	

First, cut up the veal in nice little strips. Then you can mix together the cornstarch, salt, and water, and cover the pieces veal with this paste. Make hot the oil in a frying pan and throw in the slices mushroom and the cucumber. For 3 minutes you should cook, and don't forget to stir. Then you can put in the strips veal and cook for another 7 or 8 minutes. Pour on the soy sauce, mix it in nice, and cook for 2 minutes. Now you're done and you can serve. Make more if you're fixing for more than 2 people . . . Such a flavor!

* *MEES KITE*: what they called her before the "nose job."

BARBEQUED RIBS TZEL TZUH*

2 lbs. lamb ribs cut into strips   2 teaspoons white vinegar
3 tablespoons honey   3 tablespoons duck sauce
¼ cup soy sauce   2 tablespoons oil
¼ cup ginger ale

The ribs should be cut up into not too big pieces, so with your fingers you can eat. Then you'll mix all together the other things and let the ribs marinate in them for an hour or so. After that, you'll put on a rack the ribs and put them in the oven (350°) for an hour and a quarter. You shouldn't forget to baste every once in a while. Remember, the more you baste, the better they taste. When the oven time is up put the ribs under the broiler for a minute or two, they should get nice and brown. You can serve with a little duck sauce 4 people.

* *TZEL TZUH*: the Jewish ginger ale Mr. Lipschitz delivers every Friday.

96

SAUCES, DIPS
AND SPICES

SZECHUAN SALT

A tablespoon Szechuan
   peppercorns
6 tablespoons kosher salt

In a frying pan you'll cook first the peppercorns over a
medium fire. When you're finished cooking you'll know,
because the kitchen will smell wonderful. Be careful! Don't
burn! Now the salt and the peppercorns you'll put in the
blender and blend for a few minutes. When it's done it
should be kept in a good tight jar, it should keep for a long
time. This is used for dipping or sprinkling on duck and
chicken or whatever you like.

98

FIVE SPICES POWDER

4 cinnamon sticks, 2 inches long
6 whole star anise
2 teaspoons Szechuan peppercorns
20 cloves
2 teaspoons fennel seed

All these things you should put into the blender and blend good until you have a fine powder and the kitchen it smells beautiful! What you don't use, in a tight jar you'll keep so it lasts for a long time. If you're a little lazy or maybe a liberated working housewife you can also find it in a Chinese grocery or maybe the "Gourmet" shelf in the supermarket.

GARLIC DIP

3 cloves garlic, chopped nice
A good pinch sugar
2 tablespoons light soy
A teaspoon Hot Oil

Mix good together everything and serve it in a little dish
or maybe in individual dishes. This dip is nice to dunk
pieces chicken or duck or sometimes even fish.

PLUM SAUCE

1 cup water
1 cup sugar
A 16-oz. can peaches, drained
A 16-oz. can plums, pitted and
     drained
A 1″ x 2″ piece pressed tamarind
(can be found at Indian grocery stores)

Cut up first the tamarind into small pieces and in a pot you'll put it with a cup water. This you should let cook for 5 minutes so it's soft. Put the peaches and plums into your blender together with the tamarind and blend so you have a nice purée. Now you'll pour into a saucepan the purée and stir in good the sugar. Let this simmer for 30 minutes over a low fire and every once in a while give a little stir. When it's done let it cool and it's ready to use. It makes 2½ cups and for weeks it will keep in the refrigerator.

101

HOT OIL

A cup vegetable oil
6 tablespoons powdered red pepper

Make hot in a pot the oil, so it smokes. Then you'll take off from the fire and stir in the pepper. Let it cool good and put it away in a tight bottle. A lifetime you'll have enough for because, believe me, Maalox it isn't.

102

DESSERT

GOLDEN CUSTARD ZEI
GUH ZINT*

3 fresh egg yolks	1 cup milk
½ cup flour	1 teaspoon almond extract
2 tablespoons sugar	A pot hot oil
A little cornstarch	2 more tablespoons sugar
A pinch salt	2 tablespoons grated almonds

Beat nice the egg yolks so they'll get thick. Then you'll sift together the flour with the sugar, salt and 1 tablespoon cornstarch. Pour a little of this into the egg yolks, then pour also a little milk, then a little more of the flour mixture. Keep pouring and mixing a little of each until it's all used up. Put this whole mish-mash in a double boiler and cook until it gets thick, you shouldn't forget to stir. When it's thick put in the almond extract . . . and mix. Now you'll smear a little butter all over a flat pan and the mixture you'll pour in. Cover it nice and put it in the refrigerator so it should get cold. Then you can cut into small squares and roll around in the cornstarch. Put it next into the pot hot oil and deep fry it until it gets a nice brown color. Take it out from the oil and drain thoroughly. Then mix together the sugar and almonds and roll around in it, it should cover all over. This makes enough for 4 people on high calorie diets.

(Of course you know it's not Kosher to serve this right after a meat dish. But you can serve it first . . . or 6 hrs. after a meat meal . . . but that would mean a *very* early dinner. So better you should save this dish for a fish night.)

* *ZEI GUH ZINT*: Lucrezia Borgia's favorite toast.

BANANAS MEH SHU GAH*

2 medium size bananas, sliced in chunks
6 tablespoons sugar
2 tablespoons oil

Heat in the pan a little oil and fry for 5 minutes the pieces banana. While you're frying you can heat the sugar in a pot until it melts. When the bananas are fried, into the melted sugar you should put them . . . and make sure they are all over covered. Serve them already before the sugar hardens.

On the table, in front of each person, there should be a dish cold water. Each person picks up a piece banana and dips it into the water. This makes it cool so your mouth you shouldn't burn. Be careful you don't serve this too much. From all that sugar, the teeth could fall out.

Serves 2 good customers for my son, the dentist.

* *MEH SHU GAH* refers to people who write Chinese-Kosher Cookbooks.

INDEX

113